I/O

Miller Williams Poetry Series
EDITED BY BILLY COLLINS

I/O

Madeleine Wattenberg

The University of Arkansas Press
Fayetteville
2021

ISBN: 978-1-68226-163-7
eISBN: 978-1-61075-742-3

Manufactured in the United States of America

25 24 23 22 21   5 4 3 2 1

Designed by Liz Lester

♾ The paper used in this publication meets the minimum
requirements of the American National Standard for Permanence
of Paper for Printed Library Materials Z39.48-1984.

Library of Congress Cataloging-in-Publication Data

Names: Wattenberg, Madeleine, author.
Title: I/O / Madeleine Wattenberg.
Description: Fayetteville: The University of Arkansas Press, 2021. |
Series: Miller Williams poetry series | Summary: "I/O, finalist for the
2021 Miller Williams Poetry Prize, alternates between epistolary poems
to the mythical figure Io and lyrical interrogations of science, myth,
and the historical record"—Provided by publisher.
Identifiers: LCCN 2020042467 (print) | LCCN 2020042468 (ebook) |
ISBN 9781682261637 (paperback) | ISBN 9781610757423 (ebook)
Subjects: LCGFT: Poetry.
Classification: LCC PS3623.A876 I6 2021 (print) | LCC PS3623.A876
(ebook) | DDC 813/.6—dc23
LC record available at https://lccn.loc.gov/2020042467
LC ebook record available at https://lccn.loc.gov/2020042468

Funded in part by

MILLER AND **LUCINDA WILLIAMS**
POETRY FUND

CONTENTS

SERIES EDITOR'S PREFACE

When the University of Arkansas Press invited me to be the editor of its annual publication prize named in honor of Miller Williams—the longtime director of the press and its poetry program—I was quick to accept. Since 1988, when he published my first full-length book, *The Apple That Astonished Paris*, I have felt keenly indebted to Miller. Among the improvements to the world made by Miller before his death in January 2015 at the age of eighty-four was his dedication to finding a place for new poets on the literary stage. In 1990, this commitment became official when the first Arkansas Poetry Prize was awarded. Fittingly, upon his retirement, the prize was renamed the Miller Williams Poetry Prize.

When Miller first spotted my poetry, I was forty-six years old with only two chapbooks to my name. Not a pretty sight. Miller was the one who carried me across that critical line, where the "unpublished poets" impatiently wait, and who made me, in one stroke, a "published poet." Funny, you never hear "unpublished novelist." I suppose if you were a novelist who remained unpublished you would stop writing novels. Not the case with many poets, including me.

Miller Williams was more than my first editor. Over the years, he and I became friends, but even more importantly, before I knew him, I knew his poems. His straightforward, sometimes folksy, sometimes witty, and always trenchant poems were to me models of how poems might sound and how they could *go*. He was one of the poets who showed me that humor had a legitimate place in poetry—that a poem could be humorous without being silly or merely comical. He also showed me that a plainspoken poem did not have to be imaginatively plain or short on surprises. He was one of my literary fathers.

Miller occupied a solid position on the American literary map, though considering his extensive career and steady poetic output, it's surprising that his poems don't enjoy even more prominence. As his daughter became the well-known singer and recording artist that she is today, Miller came to be known as the father of Lucinda Williams. Miller and Lucinda even appeared on stage together several times, performing a father-daughter act of song and poetry. In 1997, Miller came to the nation's attention when Bill Clinton chose him to be the inaugural poet for his second inauguration. The poem he wrote for that event, "Of History and Hope," is a meditation on how "we have memorized America." In turning to the children of our country, he broadens a nursery rhyme question by asking "how does *our* garden grow?" Miller knew that occasional poems, especially for occasions of such importance, are notoriously difficult—some would say impossible—to write with success. But he rose to that occasion and produced a winner. His confident reading of the poem before the nation added cultural and emotional weight to the morning's ceremony and lifted Miller Williams to a new level of popularity and respect.

Miller was pleased by public recognition. What poet is immune? At home one evening, spotting a headline in a newspaper that read POET BURNS TO BE HONORED, Miller's wife, Jordan, remarked, "They sure have your number." Of course, the article was about an annual celebration honoring Robert Burns.

Miller's true legacy lies in his teaching and his career as a poet, which covered four decades. In that time, he produced over a dozen books of his own poetry and literary theory. His poetic voice tends to be soft-spoken but can be humorous or bitingly mordant. The poems sound like speech running to a meter. And they show a courteous, engaging awareness of the presence of a reader. Miller knew that the idea behind a good poem is to make the reader feel something, rather than to merely display the poet's emotional state, which has a habit of boiling down to one of the many forms of misery. Miller also possessed the authority of experience to produce poems that were just plain wise.

With Miller's sensibility in mind, I set out to judge the first year's contest. I was on the lookout for poems that resembled Miller's. But the more I read, the more I realized that applying such narrow criteria would be selling Miller short and would not be fair to the entrants. It would make more sense to select manuscripts that Miller would enjoy reading for their own merits, not for their similarity to his own poems. That his tastes in poetry were broader than the territory of his own verse can be seen in the variety of the books he published. The list included poets as different from one another as John Ciardi and Jimmy Carter. Broadening my own field of judgment brought happy results, and I'm confident that Miller would enthusiastically approve of this year's selections—winner Michael McGriff's *Eternal Sentences*, finalist Craig Blais's *Moon News*, and finalist Madeleine Wattenberg's *I/O*—as well as those of previous years.

———

If I had to give a Hollywood elevator pitch on behalf of Michael McGriff's *Eternal Sentences*, the 2021 Miller Williams Poetry Prize winner, I might say that it's a blend of the low-rent sociology of Raymond Carver with the quirky imagination of Richard Brautigan. The speaker of these poems lives in the realm of Kmart, McDonald's, and Gas Qwik. Friends are in jail. A snake is coiled inside a Schlitz can, the family is too proud to accept food stamps, and the neighbors are "too poor for a fence." But that, compared to the method and power of these poems, is just the scene, not the subject.

The title of this book is very explicit about what lies inside, that is, a series of sentences. Of course, we could describe just about all writing from the Bible to Jim Thompson as a progression of sentences, but here the sentence is king. I was enjoying myself so much on first reading that I failed to notice right away the distinguishing scheme at work in every poem. Each line of every poem is its own periodic sentence, where the reader must fully stop before he or she can go on. And the period is the only punctuation allowed in this collection, apart from a handful of apostrophes just to keep track of who owns what. The comma, a useful way to guide the sentence and control its rhythm, is banned. The period rules. The deeper we wade into McGriff's collection, the more we realize that while the exclusive use of end-stopped sentences, one after the other, is the source of the poems' power, it is also a self-imposed restriction. It reminded me of W. S. Merwin's comment that he abandoned (or transcended!) punctuation in order to make writing poems more difficult for himself by doing without its help. Here, every one of McGriff's poems is a box of sentences.

Such a repetition of short, declarative sentences risks the monotony some associate with the lockstep heroic couplets of eighteenth-century English poetry. But the sentences here, for the most part, are a wonder. Whether linked to create a suggestion of a narrative or, just as commonly, to not strain toward a singular point, the stacks of sentences are always fresh and often striking. Some are straightforward:

"I wore the same jacket to your wedding and your funeral."
"My sandwich tastes worse than I thought."
"They're poking at a fire with curtain rods."

Others are quirky, surrealistic:

"A skyful of sparrows poured from my chest."
"I try to step through a mirror discarded in an alley."
"Three early stars torqued into place along the border."

And the hand of Brautigan is present:

"The elk sharpen their craft of disregarding us."
"Everyone from the eighteenth century looks seventy-five and doomed."

Eternal Sentences makes us reexamine the line in poetry and the sentences that lines can hold. Charles Olsen ordered that "no line must sleep." The lines gathered here could not be more aroused, aware, and wakeful. Here's one poem in its entirety:

Tonight I Am

A dead flashlight in a kitchen drawer.
A sheet of three-cent stamps.
A fistful of gravel as a last defense.
Wind against the house lying through its teeth.

This series of short sentences produces both individual eye-openers as well as some overlap that suggests possible patterns. One leaves these poems with the feeling that life comes at us in a series of sentences too stark to be interrupted by the brake-tapping of a comma. I've heard metaphors for life that hold less truth. *Eternal Sentences* will come at its readers as a series of happily endless delights.

———

To return to the elevator for a moment—*Moon News*, finalist for the 2021 Miller Williams Poetry Prize, can be seen as the unlikely marriage of Charles Bukowski and Sir Philip Sidney, but of course, that doesn't do justice to Craig Blais, who is a strong and engaging poet in his own right. We can say that *Moon News* is a collection of sonnets if we allow that a poem cast in the basic shape of a sonnet is a sonnet. The shadow of the English sonnet is visible here: fourteen lines divided into three quatrains and the couplet. But the quatrains are not grammatical units as they tend to be with the Elizabethans; rather, they run on into the next quatrain and finally into the couplet, amen. This is the more urgent, jumpy sonnet in which the poet talks through the shape of the poem, hurrying ahead until he feels the couplet nearing; then he finds a way to use the two remaining lines to close the poem up. As readers, we experience both the familiarity of the sonnet box and the many novel twists and odd surprises of this poet's original hand. In one poem, Blais's grandmother's pea soup recipe acts as the closing couplet. In other scenarios, the couplets sound like items from a police blotter or a nurse's log. This is the sonnet repurposed for our time.

Here's one example from a stack of endings. The speaker is sitting at home watching a football game and drinking "a thirty-pack" when a friend stops by and declares he is "interested in exploring 'traditional / masculine gender roles.'" And here are the lines that directly follow:

> The sun is reversing
>
> its magnetic field every eleven years—flipping
> end over end like a chariot tossed by horses
> off the road and down a rocky embankment.
> North becomes south and south north as it follows
>
> an orbit around a galaxy center that flails its arms
> like a wide receiver looking for a penalty flag.

That is not allowed in prose, and it shows Blais's full awareness of the high degree of imaginative freedom offered by poetry. To read these poems is to be both enclosed by the sonnet's chalk lines and released by the wildness of the content. The swerves of thought are not dictated by the sonnet's divisions. A poem that begins about a friend schooling the poet for his drinking ends this way: "Molten iron / converts to steel and hardens until the next thing // you know, there are 446 bridges in your city / and a weapon for every imaginable atrocity." Poems, it has been said, should at least be interesting—and these are in spades. Speaking of which, a woman reading tarot cards is "bluffing like she's in the middle of a poker game." The poet writes someone's phone number on a rock and tosses it into his backyard in case he ever locks himself out of his house; he does this because "I am scared."

Most poets in America teach. Blais is in the minority who

admit the experience into their poems. In teaching Kafka's *Metamorphosis*, he deals with one student who says, "'That's weird.' / The same thing he's said all semester about everything." Another thinks Gregor—the "bug-man"—"brought it on himself somehow." Or "his family did it to him." Finally, the "weird" kid is given the couplet: "'Maybe it's not about *why*. Maybe it's about / how everybody left behind just has to deal with it.'" In another poem about teaching English, the students are unimpressed when told "that *stanza* in Italian / means *room*," so teacher tells them it really means *crime scene*.

Moon News modulates into a series of sonnets about Saint Blaise, "patron saint of animals and those suffering from throat ailments." Here reverential prayers mix with hagiographic exaggerations: "Like Jesus, Blaise walked on water, but unlike Jesus, / when he got to the center of the lake, he sat down." Another section is a kind of elegy for friend "Alex," but the tone is mixed like the tone of this whole book. The sonnet never before carried such cargo: heroin, hospital rooms, poems growing out of trees and out of a person's open hand, a flower drooping "like it could give a fuck," Jeff Bezos, Tom Brady, and SpongeBob himself.

Moon News is a dazzling collection of fully American sonnets. And if you want to get the real moon news, Blais will tell you that "the moon appeared after earth took a glancing blow / off the chin 4.5 billion years ago. // Every day since it has been tugging at our seas / like a child afraid its mother will leave."

Io, you might recall, was one of the lovers of Zeus who was turned into a heifer then back into a woman. And in *I/O*, she holds a lantern to guide a poet through a book of poems, for Madeleine Wattenberg is a votary of this goddess. Io is her confidante and confessor. It is Io to whom her letters are addressed, as if the poet had one foot in the ancient world of mythology and the other in her own time. In opening up a channel between her personal history and the age of mythology, the poet develops a private association with Io and her time. *I/O* is peppered with questions as if the poet sought answers to her own unfolding journey: "Io, tell me how you left the grove." "Tell me how you crossed the sea with only a gnat for company." "Were you surprised when Hera took you into the grove and fastened your gold collar?" The poems seem to toggle back and forth between ancient and modern realms, with the ancient world dominating the sensibility and the sound of each utterance. Even when the poet is in her own time, her language sounds vaguely elemental, as if she wants to be better understood by Io. Subtle, intentional missteps in grammar and diction signal an effort to write in a more basic English with a more ancient sound. Nature is even animated as it would be in a mythological world: "The hills shift their shadows as though swinging a load from hip to hip." Her more natural language is tinged with a delicate sensuousness. She is "careful not to tear the purple skin" of a plum. She announces that "I don't wash my hair for ten straight years / and each day the oil drips down my back." And while swimming, "Underwater, my feet / glitter like pink cities." And many of Wattenberg's poems sparkle with stunningly inventive images, as when trees spread "like tails of peacocks to the sky" or "the clouds remain closed as caskets."

Another female figure enters the scene with Margaret Cavendish, the seventeenth-century poet, scientist, and pioneer feminist who published under her own name and challenged the belief in a mechanistic world. We get a view of the duchess's complex laboratory. Cavendish appears in a poem titled "Uses for Late Frost," which recalls a scene from her groundbreaking novel *The Blazing World* in which "a merchant abducts / a daughter as she gathers / shells along the shore." The lines that follow—"They sail to where two / worlds meet"—reminded me of how Wattenberg makes the two worlds of today and ancient Greece meet through the agency of Io.

For me, the poem that best represents the strange power

and imaginative pressure of this book is "Charon's Obol," in reference to the coin that those being transported to the underworld must give the ferryman. The myth serves as background and grounding wire to the poet's growing up, from her father placing on her tongue "a sliver of peach / or a white pastille . . . a homeopathic moon," to her tongue "sliding against the edges of men," including "a boy who tastes of copper." Finally, the coin becomes the obol of death. The poet practices dying by placing "a coin / across my tongue." "How can I know which boat to board," she asks in terminal confusion, "I'm just trying to pay my way." *I/O*, despite its brief title, is a book of expansive power and enviable craft.

Congratulations to all three of these poets. The University of Arkansas Press is honored to be the home for these titles for years to come.

Billy Collins

A woman in the shape of a monster
a monster in the shape of a woman
the skies are full of them

a woman   'in the snow
among the Clocks and instruments
or measuring the ground with poles'

—ADRIENNE RICH,
"Planetarium"

Except by Violence (i)

Breath   scrapes

      over   whetstone

through   the alloy   tube.

      Airstream   splits

         into   sound.

      To alter   the note

wavering   in   the hollow

      I

covered   an opening.

Dear Io,

I have to decide what happens in a room.

I take out my scissors. I rearrange the pieces until you unclasp a turquoise hair clip and hair retreats up your shoulders. A god walks away, looks away, thinks elsewhere.

Through the bedroom window, I watch a neighbor's pool rotate through the seasons. To each blossom that falls onto its turquoise surface I recite the word for time. Its surface does not look turquoise until I look away. The blossoms do not fall.

I've rearranged the letters.

The memory pulls together like liquid, like a glass of water falling to the hardwood. All the sharp edges run from each other. I find a dustpan, a cloth, a Band-Aid for the door from which a red tendril escapes across the water.

Charon's Obol

My father gave me a small jar of honey
　　　　and each night I took a secret lick.
Long after the gold hardened to granule
　　　　my tongue returned to my mouth sweet.
Later he placed between my lips a sliver of peach
　　　　or a white pastille
dissolving down—a homeopathic moon.
　　　　I kept my tongue clean beneath those gifts.

My tongue has since turned.
　　　　Sliding against the edges of men,
I wonder where that gold's gotten to
　　　　and settle for a boy who tastes of copper,
who flaps like a whiskey-watered hawk
　　　　and scatters me.
I know you don't mean it—I'd repeated,
　　　　until he refused me passage in his horror.
Empty anther. I wash him off with mint.
　　　　His sorrys fill my bed until I'm crowded out.
I count them like coin when they rattle at night.

We hope sounds will open our mouths
　　　　and force us into breath. I place a coin
across my tongue and practice dying.
　　　　In some cold places, the obol staves
return. My lips seal in the acerbic promise;

whole rivers run through me.
How can I know which boat to board—
I'm just trying to pay my way.

He removes the coin from my mouth
with his own hand. My sordid god.
But this is nothing new, this reaching into
and withdrawing. The truth is
I'd tongue the honey from most any hand
that granted me a crossing.

Dear Io,

Suppose I transpose an image of one life over another. In the first life, a ship sits low in the water. In the second life, the ship leaves the harbor without a passenger. What sound emerges from this doubling?

Only the hollow body chimes. The air rattles inside the core— a method of production. I listen to my body make pleasant sound, wonder what mouth blew this violence into me. An imperfect line in imperfect skin balances the gap. I dab with disinfectant until the red turns. A used shape—who holds the knife that makes the wound a well.

Ars Mythos

Like women, birds
             are bad news.

They come with cutting
                   vanes and steel

rachis. Hercules
             shot the Stymphalian,

but not before
             they'd shed their swords

and wormed their beaks
                   into the farmers' lush

bodies. Here every
             suffering will be made

visible or at least
             not written out.

Consider how after
             Procne's husband

rapes her sister
             she serves him their son's

flesh. One body
             entering another

in reprisal for the same.
                    All characters of this myth

live the remainder
                    of their sufferings as birds.

Sister as nightingale—
                    symbol of scored

silence. The husband
                    under the tarnished crown

of an orange-crested
                    hoopoe. Procne

transformed into a small
                    swallow, the act

of consumption. This punishment
                    requires she draw

into the cavity of her body
                    foreign pieces

of the world and let
                    them live. I reject

that I can either consume
                    or want to be

consumed, but I
            admit I admire

the raptor that desires
                another's body

to keep beneath
           her glowing field
                    of iron feathers.

Dear Io,

I ferried myself across the river until my shoulders and wrists thickened and my handprints lay deep in the oars. The journey's repetitions grew so familiar that I looked down to see my face on the water. I threw a coin and her eye rippled outward.

Field Guide to Fission

A yellow hat peaks
    over the sandbar,

then the yellow
    fishing gaiters

climb the dune.
    Next, the hand appears

holding a bucket under
    the thickest glasses

I'd ever seen.
    As I try them on

the sea goes bleary
    and orange.

"Don't shuffle
    your feet,"

says Uncle Al.
    Mud rose

in mushroom smoke
    through clear water.

"Careful of sharp
    edges," he says.

Later the Band-Aid
        floated on the surface.

While we eye the coast
        for signs of buried life,

Uncle Al tells me
        about his favorite

professor from college—
        an Italian called Fermi.

Together they played
        on the squash courts

under the university and formed
        a successful atomic volley.

"His wife was Jewish
        like us," says Uncle Al.

Underwater, my feet
        glitter like pink cities.

We look for breathing
        holes, puckers of white

sand surrounded by black
        sand. I scuttle

from a red crab.
     He picks it

up by its pincers.
     "Should we drop it

in with the others?"
     he asks.

He does and the whole
     world shudders.

Dear Io,

I have managed to not ask you. The sun rose out of the cherry trees this morning.

Dear Io,

I squint in the bathroom mirror and in my iodine-splashed skin see a bronze statue. If rain fell, I would chime. The clouds remain closed as caskets. It does not rain. I would meet myself again to make that wind-begotten sound. I will make myself again to be that air meeting metal. When I lean on my hands and knees to sponge the spackled floor, I find a fly suspended at the center of an amber drop.

Poem in Which the Trojan Horse Burns Blue

On the wine-darkened carpet, I'm waiting
for a new word that allows me to depart
from this room. Until then, I use other
makeshift horses. Like that ship in a bottle
you crookedly glued. It wants to be tinder,
easily ignites. What left but to throw it
in the fireplace and watch the glass collapse.
The beauty of fire resides in its insistence
on leaving something behind. A shadow
or ash fleck harbored in the lung. Heat.
I don't wash my hair for ten straight years
and each day the oil drips down my back,
a just-in-case gasoline that I keep close by.
I'll bring you to your knees by any means,
any pyre, any invocation to combustion.
I learn new forms for measuring the sea;
by sand grain, salt grain, driftwood, or knot—
how many blushed pearls to launch a single
fist? I split my voice into a chorus to drive you
from your ship's wood hull. Like fire, the sea
appears red or blue according to the length
of time that it has burned. When I utter *our,*
you mistake it for *war.* So we build our ships
again, face the terrible shores of each other.

Dear Io,

I dragged the fly out by a wing. I pushed a toothpick through
the hinge of it. O,

I said, as though someone holding a harp would hear me and
take it from my hand.

Io,

In myth, every celestial object forms a portal to deliver you back
to your story. I jump through their bodies—this one, this one,
this one. Ice, onyx, glass. In myth, glass is a liquid compelled by
gravity toward the windowsill. We glisten on the bed like statues.
We wait to be drawn beyond gravity. I take a walk through the
neighborhood and count how many others close their fingers
around the air as though oars have appeared there.

Invocation to Flame

Though the gods have been carried off   like slivers of ash
      I still strike up my word   In this prayer,
the piece of coal   can't decide whether to burn   or be burned
      or if tomorrow the verb will matter   In this prayer,
you are next to me   and we stare at the trees' bodies
      made to make smoke   In this prayer   I pray nothing
else transforms   because if you see smoke   something
      made it through   fire without breaking   In this
prayer, it's okay   that what heals   hardens
      In this prayer, I don't ask you to touch me
but I do ask you to string my name   from your teeth
      In this prayer, you ask   a question   Isn't it strange?
But then you fade into the dark   so this prayer
      is like the others   In this prayer, the woods watch
lightless as a closed hand   In this prayer,

      the wind shifts direction   and I repeat myself

because repetition is as close   as memory comes
      to its cremation   In this prayer, though gunfire
In this prayer, though bullet   In this prayer, though red iron
      my language won't cauterize   In this prayer, there
are ways other   than first nothing, then pain
                    to measure the body.

Flute

In the dark, the olive tree
could be the plum
tree I knew
as a girl or the tail
of a peafowl dragging
dust through the yard.
New limbs hang
salt-strung and sore.
I hear him close
and open
his body.
Now dust
riddles me.
I have learned
men guard women
for other men
and greet
each other with knives
at their hips
and sing war songs
while thinning the blades.

Dear Io,

The fly fell on me like I was sugar. Whispered saccharine epithets into my ear: sweet-tongued Io, milk-river Io, Io of the honeycomb body. Be not wary of the tongues of gods. Glory to she who succumbs. I abandoned the washing. I left the river to its run. The fly rubs grains of salt across my skin. Says openness is its own reward.

As a daughter, I never strayed. Mother never stopped watching for me. In summer, we picked plums. Father went to work before the flies rose and came home after they had died for the day. They hummed low to our picking. Plums slipped from our fingers, swallowed by the baskets. Later we cleaned them, Mother holding the pieces underwater. I was careful not to tear the purple skin with the polishing rag. At night, against the trees spreading like tails of peacocks to the sky, Father's car slunk home. Her whole life, Mother never stopped tasting the white gravel road.

I hear his eyes blink shut: drawers closing, paper falling, wings closing back on the body. The tree becomes a circle becomes a track becomes a way of becoming. Their leaves rustle: pages and doors drawing, turning, arms pulled to the chest. I sense my body shifting under the skin. Where have my hands gone. How to hold now to anything. He closes half his eyes and opens the others.

Eye-city. Eyes from the windows, the towers, the walls. Body pulled through windows, stretched across flanks, down fetlock, hock. Harden into hoof. Cower, or coward, these streets belong to the boys with heavy-lidded eyes.

I smelled coarse as clove. I never hid. Hide became the thing I wore. He flew upon me. Flies always liked me best. I've transformed. He transformed me. I don't know my own mind. I raised my hands, but the light obscured them down to the wrist.

The aperture resists full focus in anything but complete and perfect light, so you must at all times choose what to take with you.

Io,

I was just a little unclean when he dressed me in the bride's cloth. Did the veil also weigh your spine until you crouched to the floor on hard fists? Gold poked like two horns from my crown.

Were you surprised when Hera took you into the grove and fastened your gold collar? I imagine her reaching with a god-like finger to give the bell a hard flick, its endless metal ring an accompaniment to her leaving.

Io,

Tell me about crossing the sea in a ship. How the waves rocked your changed body until the entire ocean lay still as glass and the land jolted white. Lay still as—

Dear Io,

You knew in the gods' score each note was a body littered across the lines, each body defined by the silence lying to either side of its head. I think of you when this body blinks out.

The Shivering Fancy turns
To a fictitious Country

—EMILY DICKINSON

Imprint with Need

Beneath the transparent sheet
of your chest runs a blue story:
a child and a child

don't know that need
is a season to prepare for.
I tell the doctors

there are things in your body
not worth finding,

a self-administered
shadow.

Months twist
into hoary hours.

You took down the ladder
that once took us
to the roof.

We grew into the red house.

We called each other every name we knew
for winter.

The rope swing
hangs above the gray
lawn in knots.

Cool for the skin's distance
from blood, I taste your fever
with the back of my hand.

A palm's heat confuses
and palm to palm we lived,
until you pierced your skin
with that needle
full of northern winds.

You closed your body
to how you were made.

In deep December,
fish swim
restricted strata.
Ice grows over them,
a still, white trellis.

The marriage and divorce
of it. It drips back
into water.

A vision of summer
oxidized our wet lungs.

Too cold, we said.
The world
was slowing.

Ice creaks inside the birdbath—
Imagine the moment you decide to go
is already the moment you've gone.

Reconfiguration

Where the bird used to land—

        I've been told not to look

there anymore, that every migration

        repeats itself as a vacancy

on the branch. And it's true

        the leaf travels to the ground,

bark edges out the blades,

        black branches cradle a solid

sky. This balance between foreground

        and birdcall. This memory

a wing fled somewhere warm.

        And maybe this advice is right,

that the body removed from the figure

        and safe from the prisms of frost

lasts longer by the shore. Yet in emptiness

        the trees look full now,

so full the sky seems poised to break

        every raised hand it rests in.

An Inventory of Margaret Cavendish's Laboratory

An outside. An inside.

One can assume salt in a rough wet mouth.

Her father's house was not far from the sea.

An orange removed from under the hand's heel—

pressure at two poles.

A cut in the damp air. Light like a rind crescent.

It is impossible to round this world.

The boats ride on the waves in a geometry

of hollowed cells. *Honeycomb.*

A scientific animal. A crushed telescope.

Charcoal. Pipette nettle.

A privation of light. A fiction rattles in the centrifuge.

Bear-men. Bird-men. An emperor.

A bowl of seeds and a scalpel. A hypothesis.

A particular part cannot increase of itself.

The frozen men on long silver counters.

Cross-sections of stone.

Graf Zeppelin over Siberia

Beneath the body lie packed fields of snow,
blue molecules grinding to silence, white
ridges. Where gray convenes, disjointed mountains
rise from the tundra's flank. And we rise too,
or are risen, the body's shadow clinging
like ice to stern. Through corridors, canals
of ushered light, we breathe complacently
ascending hollow as a silver cup
to the sky's metallic mouth. Illusive vessel.

I count the days that pass in this dusk.
The sun casts placid glances against the cold.
If we are the short day, both sun and shade,
both port and passage, we neither cease to turn
nor press ourselves to motion. Rotation keeps us
where we belong. The villagers look up
and pray. They've fallen to their knees. For one
moment we circle them, our solid body
a blot, a blight, then gone. The winter's hard
as winter. The elk still scuff the permafrost
for thrusts of roots. The villagers return
to stone or snow. From here, we can't discern
so deeply frozen. We don't know the length
thaw runs or how to turn the mind
back. It could be a thousand feet below
the people build their homes from clouds. What color
is coldest when its space allows. What distance.

The engine's hum reminds the passengers
of what they once called wind. Donning furs,
they appear like arctic foxes peeping out
of the ports. The mountains grow from dusty hills.
We barely clear the peaks, the pinnacles
conspire toward our bloated shape. A prick—
the white horizon folds itself in half
just to press a point. And then we glide
beyond the tundra—tips of green, the taiga
rushes upward and our body flushes with color.

The Blazing Field

A pocketknife rattles in the washing machine.
Spring hasn't yet broken through.
After we attend a lecture on circumbinary planets,
you take me to the astronomy tower.
On a wobbly stool,
I look at the rings of Saturn,
a planet named for the god who eats his sons
in fear they will defeat him.
In the circumference of my doubled eye,
the planet, surrounded by the black iris
of a universe, blushes.
How much closer will you come?
The quiet ceded by the tower's retractable roof
solidifies. When I step away from the eyepiece,
a circular impression
around my right eye begins to fade.
The machine clunks to the end of its cycle.

—

The universe had to create itself—you say. I inhale a blend of Old
Spice and Dove. One of our watches ticks on a quarter-second
delay. *Nothing was unstable,* you say. *Let me rephrase:* nothing
was stable.

—

On our kitchen table,
a plum nearing the end

of ripeness, stretched
around a near-sphere

of purple ice.
At the center, a seed

an echo of the fruit
from which fruit erupted.

———

It threw itself apart. What we see of light is not enough.

———

*What happened was nothing split in two—negative nothing,
positive nothing—until, unstable, nothingness threw itself apart.*
Rain riddles the window. Your equations cross the whiteboard
like bird feet in snow. How far did you go in the space between
our minds? Did you enter the universe's reflection? Did you let
the ancient waves scatter to pigment in your new blue eye? But
what about the *very* beginning? *Don't ask,* you say. *There was no
time. You cannot imagine it.* Blue as the lightless space between
our planet and the one you return your eye to in the dark.

We built a home in the field of swinging debris.

———

Two gold cubes on a scale—

how do you make one weigh more than the other

without addition or subtraction?

———

All night the sky performs its old ceremony. You return in the mornings with rings around your eyes. At the horizon, the husband hesitates, then thumbs his new bride's hem. I pick at crumbs, place a plate of them before you, and soon they turn to toast, to over easy, to a bowl full of bright tangerines.

———

Imagine medusa *floating in space*

in static configuration. The repulsive

force between medusa *and earth*

would disavow their mutual attraction

and she would float where stone floats.

———

Two horizons, having never met, share a nearly identical heat.

On the nights you stay home with fever, I let myself reside in it. We sleep heavily and our bodies curl like smoke. I leave a glass of water by the bed. Fever is a trickster. We pay homage to our false cold.

Medusa sleeps and a strand of her hair opens

its mouth and licks my elbow. It is dreaming
that a three-headed dog chases its singular tail

and metal birds clatter from the sky.

Warm flows into cold. Pages grow beneath my dry fingerprints.

———

Men will be birds. Stars will have tails. *The sun has a solid and fixéd body*, the birds conclude.

———

Broken orbits lead to broken things,

so we paused to watch the wreck,

two pieces of tinder in the blazing field.

Viewed closer, the sun loses shape,

becomes a vaporous lilac bloom,

becomes the hot face of nothing.

———

I measure coffee grounds and watch the water drip through the filter. The filter darkens. Mismeasured water dribbles over the lip. *If you heat up a cube, the molecules in motion grow heavy with new energy and the scale tips to their favor.* Is this not a matter of justice? A sword pares myth from fact. Justice equals two cold cubes evenly weighted.

I set your coffee beside the piled papers and pick the fuller cup up.

———

We left that stolen-fire
center
as two cooling stones.

Uses for Late Frost

Isn't every world built
for experiment?
This world is already
a laboratory on fire,
but we can practice
putting ice to good use,
press it to the newly
acquired burn

because winter still holds
on by its fingernails.
The imprint lasts,
but it won't last
forever. May as well
make it useful,

watch ice transform
skin to emptied
honeycomb
through a movement
as simple
as touch.

In Cavendish's *The Blazing World,*
a merchant abducts
a daughter as she gathers
shells along the shore.
They sail to where two
worlds meet.

The men freeze
into silence
in the ship's cabin.
Imagine her loneliness
as she travels like sand
through that hourglass's
narrow waist.

And her joy.
Cavendish knew
that by framing it as fancy
she could complete
this winter's science.
Here is the boat, she says,
I swear it is only
an act of the imagination.

At last, the Boat still passing on,
was forced into another World.

—MARGARET CAVENDISH

Dear Io,

This morning a glass sun rose over the cherry blossoms.

Dear Io,

This morning the sun rose through cherry blossoms.

Io,

I held a match to this music but found myself holding a match
to my own hair.

I,   O,
        your name an assertion of presence negated by
        exclamation—

Dear rust river,

Dear blood moon,

Dear iodine stain,

Io,

Tell me how you crossed the sea with only a gnat for company. Tell me how you crossed the sea. I imagine wooden ships bobbing by the dock. Many eyes must have wept an ocean to see you and you must have sailed the ocean of tears shed in their pity for you. I don't think you can truly pity someone you have never met, just a vague ghost as it traverses your mind. You must have been horrified at their pity after wanting only a recessional of shells. Io, I pity you.

Io,

The current plucks at the warmth strung in my skin. I admit I left gifts for his wife. Even after. Even after he saw me kneeling on the bathroom stairs. After he carried me past the incriminating altar and through the red trees. Now both our fathers remain buried in their predictions.

Osteoclasts

I.

Our bones remodel themselves all the time, my father says
through the phone. He is explaining to me how

deer lose their antlers each spring and people break
their knees and hips. Recently, I have thought of changing

my hair and my attitude toward the person I love.
He sleeps far away from me now, and it would be less trouble

if my bones would rearrange him out of me. It is a relief
to hear this may be possible. *The word comes from Greek, klastos,*

broken, he says. We don't notice small fractures in our lives
unless it is too late. Yet the way my father talks it is as though

no body is afraid of itself. I take comfort in knowing that part
of me is made for self-destruction.

II.

When my mother takes the phone she talks of osteoporosis.
She worries for my sister and herself and their unrepairable

bones. She means their bones have lost mass. At twenty-five,
my mother stopped drinking alcohol. I am now twenty-five.

I didn't like who I was, she says, *who knows why your father stuck*
with me. I drink rarely and only in company. The man I loved

consumes himself far away from me now, yet I stay
cluttered by him. My mother reminds me to drink calcium.

But you are not built like your sister or like me, she says. I reject
alcohol in the way I imagine poison ought to be rejected.

It reassures her that I am built like my father, who waited
until she could choose him over her desire for apathy.

My mother once fractured her wrist falling off her bike.
My mother once fractured her fibula from a long run.

My mother once fractured her spine from lifting the weight
of a patient who slipped and couldn't pick herself up.

I should have known better, my mother said of her method.
As a physical therapist, she realizes the limits of her arms

and legs, but the doctors inform her that she has lost
too much and her fractures will never fuse. *I've started*

running again. Sound needs a body to travel through.
Over the line, her voice holds whole and smooth.

Echeneis, or Six Ways of Letting Go

> *Eche'neis: The Remora, or Sucking-fish,*
> *which has on the crown of its head an oblong*
> *flat disk, or sucker, by means of which it can*
> *adhere to foreign bodies.*
> *from Greek: (to hold + ship)*
>
> —Oxford English Dictionary

I.

He asks if I'm a good swimmer.
I know enough to keep my head
above water. In the dark, movement matters
more than form. He swims under
and I disperse the surface.
When we meet the sailboat (him
ahead) I reach for a railing
until my joints drop loose
and down. How simply the lake
welcomes me, until I can't tell the difference
between failure and return.

The boat rotates on her tether.
Blood flows gently as orchids from my arms,
and I am cold with the asking:
how long can we carry
our own bodies,
this heavy, private weight.

II.

Slick with the imagining of
a body that knows how to keep.

Little slack-jawed remora
hidden in the eddies,
looking for something to adhere to
in the slippage of seaweed.

A ship swallows
itself at the horizon.

III.

To hold, to hold the ship
delay, darling, delay. I'm consuming time
and you, always pushing onward, so swift
and intent, and me, a hand always drawing you
back. The ship never meant
to not know time or movement, so immersed
that they drip from her sides, yet here kept apart
by the latch of a slat mouth.
I have no arms to throw against your hull,
but find me at the rudder sucking marrow.
Blame me not for your defeat, Antony.
Caligula passed only with my attention
on that long journey. Leave me in the brine

to lash against sediment. Half-hearted cartilage,
　　we're young. Before you cross on
to the shore, delay. The dry voice of sand
　　grinding down to its final cause. Clamp
and hold. Now only yielding eddies. Only favored winds.

IV.

I let go. You go on.
I let go. You go on in a green boat.
I let go. You go on in a green boat toward a green shore.
I let go. You go on in a green boat toward a green shore and
　　when you turned
I let go. You go on in a green boat toward a green shore and
　　when you turned it was to make sure you'd left none
　　of the parts
I let go. You go on in a green boat toward a green shore and
　　when you turned it was to make sure you'd left none
　　of the parts of yourself, not even an outline of what
I let go. You go on in a green boat toward a green shore and
　　when you turned it was to make sure you'd left none
　　of the parts of yourself, not even an outline of what
　　hovers over the glass waves, the watery threshold
　　holding, holding, held, a hand
I let go.

V.

In the sailboat cabin, we raid the kitchen,
filling our hands with paper towels,
hammers, handles, until we've run out
of objects. I set aside the bottle of kerosene.
We are looking for wine.
We are looking for a way to run out
of things to hold.

The boat empties
for us and still we search. We remove
the roof, the slats, the little hinged counter.
Platter and cup. Everything—touched.

I grow tired of acceptance
and the stars' fabricated gloss
through shallow waters. But this too I accept
as fact, that even a body's reflection
rests its weight on this world.

VI.

The remora is lazy,
unbelonging
to the motion in which it takes part,
unspooling from its mouth
a secret chain
to wrap around the beloved.

To unfasten, it must catch the motion,
surpass the object.

Ghost flesh carved
from scale, a glint
of bitten shadow.

To strengthen its grip, the remora
slides into the past.

Aphagia

When I visit my father in his lab,
he instructs me not to touch anything;

the cells divide in their dishes,
the pipettes clink on the trays.

He shows me a cell under
the microscope, but the image

blurs at my hand's turn.
He says I'm watching autophagy,

the breakdown of a diseased body.
I can't focus the machine.

I forget what he has told me,
how many cells we're made of,

how, to escape the draft for Vietnam,
he filled his stomach with only water,

until, at one hundred forty-five pounds
and lightheaded, he rose from his exam seat.

I know that when Germany sent
airships they split in the wind

or consumed themselves, like acids
biting through the intestinal lining.

Before we leave the sterile lab,
my father feeds his hungry cells

three drops of reddened sugar.

Helium

If Helios had begat a daughter, if
she'd asked to take his oiled reins, and if

he had refused her, saying helium
must fill her body, that her helium mind

would make her hands too soft to use
the metal on the horses' tongues;

if she took his horses anyway
and kept them trotting to a perfect curve,

would he forgive her as he did his son?
Her father's shredded by rays—she sees

the light particles divided by his teeth.
He asks again. But what is he asking?

She could not lose control, the helium
dispersing slowly through wind-blown

thoughts. Below, a dirigible bursts and burns.
She tries to catch his words before they're gone.

The horses rustle in their harnesses.

Poem for the Father outside the Poem

At the threshold to Papa's lab, by the emergency eye shower,
    he tells me not to touch
anything. I am five years old and there is so much that I don't
    know where to start. When

he turns away, I twist from this large silver garden a plastic
    yellow test tube cap and hide it
in the safest place, between all the future words I'll speak.
    The centrifuge whirs as it separates

while vials reflect across the countertops. Papa places me
    in a chair and spins it.
I learn I am nothing to separate as blood presses against
    my skull. But when Papa sees

a yellow glint through the gap in my teeth, he pulls the cap
    from my mouth. It sits, a tooth-
marked sun, at his palm's center. And here are the obvious
    allusions—a fruit bitten

in a garden, a tongued coin for the ferryman, an unripe word
    pulled from the daughter's lips.
Yet who else would attempt to stall the sun's rotation
    to keep me whole?

Language's Anatomy

On your father's altar, you lay out the letters.
You line them up like lovers.
You line them up according to use.
You arrange their bodies in the shape of an ear.
This language has taken up a sword.
This language has drawn blood.
I want to hear you, but the drumbeat fades
and the flag of Mars advances on the field.
When they say our language went to war,
they mean it lived outside your words' reach.
By spring, poppies invade your bootprints.

Consumption Triptych

I. Irene in the Portside Dining Room

Glasses spill
        when the spine tilts
past ten degrees,
        so the captain keeps
the clothed tables
        steady under seven,
the airship anchored
        in rolling oxygen.
Soup is served
        with silver ladles,
sole with parsley
        paired with a shivering
champagne flute.
        Cream and pear
complete the courses,
        and the passengers retire
or remove themselves
        to the smoking salon.
The *Hindenburg* doesn't hurry
        the hungry palate.
In a blue vase
        over the Atlantic,
carnations and chrysanthemums.
        No stirring our progress.
Think of that taste,
        such tart emptiness,
how it falls like flame
        and catches on your tongue.

II. *Matilde at the Starboard Window*

Paralyzed on the fire escape, I watch
Matilde pause at a sill of air to count
her children. They are gathered in the burning
      lung. A sky glistens.

This city won't hold a stranger. An alarm
sounds from the roof and metal warms to my hands.
Matilde practices the transformation
      of heat into life,

dropping her boys through the window, allowing
them to fall away, little bodies of rain.
I worry my body will let go of me.
      My lungs are two fists

swinging at my chest. A looming black thorax,
Manhattan breathes out as I attempt to rise.
I'm poised between nothings, and coldly laddered
      in inconsequence,

opening fingers to the oxidized rung,
while Matilde wipes fire from her child's cheek
and lifts him through the portal, squeezing her hands
      before letting go.

III. Margot in the Lair

On the abandoned bed of a lost school,
the wolf's taste tester samples asparagus,
fresh fruit, semolina dumplings, opening
the esophagus to this one-plate portion.
To make a trap of the body, she knows
how to lure the poisonous possibility inside.
She raises her fork. But no foreign object
will eternally inhabit her.

                    Later, cyanide
or a silver bullet instead seeks his mouth—he
will administer his own end. Margot lifts her
fork, but silver kills instead the fearful man
who drags his bone plate in front of a girl
and orders her to eat before taking his bite.

Elegy for Escaped Aerostat

No one brought her down; we just watched
helium seeping out of her seams and thrilled

at her dragging tethers, wiping out electric lines
as they whipped along the roads and fields.

Some people, left powerless, trailed her
along the coast until she disappeared

into the edge of the ravine. Draped over
trees—the first time we'd seen the sky

let itself down. What filled her
to lead her to that rocky place. Where

was she going, air-backed, freely broken,
at an unclaimed cost, yet military made.

Though no one brought her down, we
would have, because isn't every unmanned

body a threat, every unshot surface
an unclaimed skin, and isn't this why we love

to hunt what runs loose over our land.

Those that withstand illnesses and predators . . .
over the winter seem impossible to destroy,
except by violence.

—FLANNERY O'CONNOR,
"Living with a Peacock"

Dear Io,

He pushed my palms into the earth. On all fours, the horizon disappears entirely. Or perhaps I merely closed my eyes. There is a river where you don't remember what you asked for, only the smell of damp soil so far from the iron odor that washes your muscles and organs.

Io,

Sometimes I close one eye. The image jumps from right to left, all but the slivered middle. Under the tree, I do this for hours, to consider how, at any given time, Argus possesses up to a hundred jumping pictures. Some are chipped, covered by an eyelash. Some echo with cataracts. He can't help where they look, so that he's always examining the dirt underfoot or inspecting the cracks in the wall at his back. We can slow the light. It just takes passing through the right state of matter.

Io,

The myth says that as the fly chases you, you cannot rest two nights in one place. Even the landscape suffers insomnia. The hills shift their shadows as though swinging a load from hip to hip.

(Re)

A girl reduced
to a thin wind
recalls
his burning
petals
floating on water
like a regression
of blades.

What does Narcissus do at night?
Doesn't his reflection
require the sun?

If he can put away his mind
in the dark hours,
I envy him.

I use a knife
in the kitchen—
every object divisible
by one
sharp thought.

I'm afraid to admit
I am afraid.

Neighbors rumble
through the walls.

A man stirs
in sleep toward his
darkness. Mine
looks back
and repeats me.

I am afraid.
I am afraid.

Dear Io,

For happiness, I sacrificed a cutting of my hair. I left the offering burning in the branches.

Io,

I've leaned heavily on images this year. I turn to the roadside copse, branches stitched over the rumble strips, while a truck bright as a flute's ribs carves its way into the side of the night. Herds of cattle graze sickish and gold. It's easier to think of myself as a marble with a field in it, a glass slope, but sometimes the image looks inward and routs me out. The corn I drive past isn't edible, but every summer it thickens its pyrite kernels.

Io,

The half-moon rose vacant as a shell.

Io,

The letter eats itself in the mirror. Dear Eye,

Shh. No one waits for you. The blinds are drawn. You open only to the cold side of the universe. No one waits for you.

What Happens in a Room

In night's throat
    I teach myself

to cut the light, to sleep
    open, to stuff hollows

with stillness. Swallow:
    a small motion,

to allow to pass
    down. Not everything

will wake up this morning.
    I want this to mean

the darkness renders
    recognition,

but too soon the room
    quickens,

first the window growing
    like an orchard on the wall,

then corners seizing
    convergence.

Daylight enters,
    paining the iris

into constricting the eye.
    To accept into

or to envelop.
    To receive, as evening

does morning,
    without question.

List of Forgotten Hinges

between river and riverbed
jaw, elbow, eyelid
between body and wing
between wick and flame
horizon, tree line, shore
bookspine, border, root
between breath and lip
between hello and goodbye
between speech and song
between sign and paper
and the tossed coin's two sides
between then and now
the moon slipping past the window
the window slipping past the moon

Dear Io,

The images retire. I cast out a net for them—harnessed only the tan carpet, four imperfect walls crossed with time and body and light.

Dear Io,

No one watches anymore. I can only compare lightning to the cherry tree's black wintered branch. I held a match to this branch but found myself holding a match to my own hair. The next day the sun rises over the trees. The wind chime shivers. The silver rods separate and fall quiet. Io, tell me how you left the grove. After every eye closed, did you linger in that shade? Io, I

lingered there.

Poem with a Penny Underneath

You were told copper turns the kiss blue,
so you put in a cent and crank the handle.
Our home is a floral mirage in a cement
glacier and our hydrangeas always grow
red. When you moved here from a distant
garden, you expected to see an iteration
of yourself on each city surface. Instead,
you watch the flowers redden and tell me
a theory about planting a penny to turn
the blooms indigo. I preferred to wander
the thin lines of city sidewalks in search
of an end that could open itself. Cities
move, if always toward failure. Two-faced,
you call me, when I return, as though
I've made a pretense of our life together.
I walk by your pile of dirt, copper singing
in its new grave. My face flushes and you
look down. The city buds silver in spring.
This continual want of what's on the other
side, it's like a penny in the sheets, isn't it—
a bruise in the shape of a president's head.
The flower head will never burn blue.
I know this as myth—the work of an ocean
over a useless treasure.

Poem in Which the Sphinx Moth Is Again Mistaken for a Hummingbird and Myth for Science

Because damp from re-
riddling the body; because hover and split
tongued; because side-step,

and this new formula
might contain a new answer. Once horned, now
pulsing fluid;

where the utterance
invades the pollen, and a long-tubed tongue
reaches the nectar.

Because the body
conforms to need—one footed, two footed, three.
The riddle changes

because the body
must ask its questions before it's too late for inquiry
and wing

thickens to wing.
But the moth heart runs the length of your body
and the morning

eye rises jaundiced
and bright over the flower lid, so you drink
while the predator

catches his breath.

Dear Io,

After a battle, feathers divide into strata. The body can be rearranged. Mineral watermarks observe from the ceiling. An eye. A city. A satellite. A crown.

Io,

I scattered grains across a city garden and didn't wait for them to breach. We have to decide if we are to blame each other now or look elsewhere.

Coin Toss

The center of
    your eye:

locus amoenus,
    tender green.

My hands come
    back to me

cupping flooded
    stories. Questions

are wedged under
    the nails like

little threats.
    Breathing

the memory
    requires my body

keep its violence,
    the pleasant

made pleasant
    for this keeping.

A periphery remains
    only to hone

the vision. There's a rule
    to keeping

a coin's two sides
    from overflowing:

one side must always wait
    for the other

to complete its turn.

Name

But as it was, all she could do was furrow
The dust with one forefoot, and make an I,
And then an O beside it, spelling her name

—Ovid's *Metamorphoses*
trans. Rolfe Humphries

While her useless father mourns
    his own godliness, death's door

eternally locked before him, mourns the way
    his daughter's new body splinters his chance

for many arrow-shaped grandsons, while he
    mourns time, jagged and incomplete,

her appeal floats formless past her tongue.
    A woman's story means little syllables

degrading as they traverse from the mind
    to newly fleshed-in thickets.

How could we expect her name to hold her
    to what we knew of her before?

Still she folded her body to create
    the letters. An unnatural body naturally bent.

Extended foreleg and the muscle's unforgiving
    forward motion. Hoof hard and angled

as a quill's nib. The letters' impossible shapes.
Three brief lines. Circle. Name

quickened in dust.

The wind blows.
The wind's blows.

Except by Violence (ii)

A door   scrapes

         over   stone

through   to the   alley.

         Air   splits

         into   song.

        I

pen   this closure

        to alter the *no*

voiced in   a room—

ACKNOWLEDGMENTS

Much gratitude for the support of the following journals in which some of these poems, in current and altered forms, first appeared: "Charon's Obol" in *Guernica*, November 2015; excerpt from "Dear Io" in *Whiskey Island* as "Aperture," Fall 2016; "*Graf Zeppelin* over Siberia" and "Matilde at the Starboard Window" in *Mid-American Review*, Spring 2016; "Invocation to Flame" and "Echeneis, or Six Ways of Letting Go" in *Muzzle Magazine*, Fall 2016; "Elegy for Escaped Aerostat" in *Devil's Lake*, Summer 2016; "What Happens in a Room" in *Ninth Letter* as "Elegy," Spring 2016; "Ars Mythos" in *Tinderbox Poetry Journal*, September 2017, and in *Best New Poets 2017: 50 Poems from Emerging Writers*, guest edited by Natalie Diaz; "An Inventory of Margaret Cavendish's Laboratory" in *Glass: A Journal of Poetry*, guest edited by Rosebud Ben-Oni, November 2017; "Reconfiguration" in the *Baltimore Review*, Fall 2017; excerpt from "Dear Io" in the *Seattle Review*, Issue 10.1, 2018; "Osteoclasts" in *Sixth Finch*, Fall 2018; "Imprint with Need" in *Puerto del Sol*, Spring 2019; and "Poem in Which the Trojan Horse Burns Blue" in *The Rumpus*, August 2019.

To the professors who have held doors open along the way, especially Jennifer Atkinson, John Drury, Sally Keith, Rebecca Lindenberg, Eric Pankey, and Lisa Williams—thank you.

Many have marked this book for the better. Thank you to my cohort and friends at George Mason University: Danielle Badra, Ben Brezner, Frank Harder, Douglas Luman, Holly Mason, Ben Renne, Melanie Tague, and Qinglan Wang; and to my IHOP family: Kristen Brida, Rhōdes Huyett, and Alexandria Petrassi.

And thank you to my beloved cohort and friends at University of Cincinnati: Lisa Ampleman, Emily Rose Cole, Cara Dees, Kimberly Grey, Sakinah Hofler, Rochelle Hurt, Toni Judnitch, Yalie Kamara, Claire Kortyna, Lisa Low, Maggie Su, Chelsea Whitton, and Matthew Yeager.

To friends, for conversations: Khunsa Amin, Andrew Hornstra, and Hannah Rose Neuhauser.

To family—Isabelle and Max Wattenberg, Nicole Sikora. Finally, to my parents Binks Wattenberg, on whose real laboratory my imaginary one depends, and Jill Miller. I love you.

NOTES

In "The Blazing Field" the analogy of the golden cube and description of Einstein's cosmological constant is drawn from Brian Greene's *The Fabric of the Cosmos* (Alfred A. Knopf, 2003).

"An Inventory of Margaret Cavendish's Laboratory" and "The Blazing Field" contain text pulled from Margaret Cavendish's *The Blazing World* (1666).

The title "Except by Violence" is taken from Flannery O'Connor's essay "Living with a Peacock."

"Matilde at the Starboard Window" recounts the story of a mother who saved her children as the *Hindenburg* exploded by dropping them out of a window.

"Margot in the Lair" refers to Margot Wölk, the only one of Hitler's fifteen taste testers to survive World War II.